OUT IN THE ALL OF IT

CHRIS HONORÉ

iUniverse, Inc.
Bloomington

Out in the All of It

iUniverse books may be ordered through booksellers or by contacting:

iUniverse
1663 Liberty Drive
Bloomington, IN 47403
www.iuniverse.com
1-800-Authors (1-800-288-4677)

ISBN: 978-1-4502-8573-5 (sc)
ISBN: 978-1-4502-8574-2 (e)

Printed in the United States of America

iUniverse rev. date: 2/17/2011

For my wife Judi, who has, with patience and good humor and love, listened to the stories, such as they are.

AUTHOR'S NOTE

Though the Peace Corps experience spans two years, the stories in this collection are taken from the first year in-country when, as a volunteer, I was a "stranger in a strange land." While the Peace Corps made every effort to prepare me – there were countless hours of language training, long afternoons on the field of play, deliberative discussions about the host country's history and traditions, all framed by the phenomenon known as culture shock – the weeks and months that followed my arrival became a personal challenge unlike anything I could ever have anticipated. The vignettes that follow are about that challenge.

If there is a genre for these stories, it could be called creative nonfiction or fictional memoir. All of the narratives are, however, based on actual experiences and capture, if not the exact time or place or person, truths that I will never forget.

PROLOGUE

It was late March, 1962. I was on the U.C. Berkeley campus, walking alone, on my way to a north side café to meet friends.

Above the road, in the distance, stood a magnificent stone and timber residence hall with a stretching athletic field. On any given day there were students playing on the field, tossing footballs and Frisbees, the street always busy, people walking to class.

On this day I saw no one. It was eerily quiet.

Then, around a soft bend in the road, came four cars headed in my direction. A small motorcade. Two police cars led the way, their lights flashing, with one unmarked sedan further back. They bracketed a gleaming black Lincoln convertible with its top down.

Curious, I waited, watching, as the Lincoln drew near. To my amazement, seated in the back of that imposing car was President Kennedy, his shock of familiar thick hair brushed by the wind. He was, I remembered, scheduled to speak at Memorial Stadium for the university's Charter Day.

Looking back, thinking about all that has happened since, I can't imagine why I was so completely ignored, one solitary individual standing on a sidewalk on a two-lane road. But that seismic day in Dallas was still more than a year away.

As the motorcade drew parallel, I told myself I wouldn't react. I'd remain cool, detached. I certainly wouldn't wave; yet there I was, one arm up in the air, waving excitedly. And then, unexpectedly, he looked directly at me, our eyes locked ever so briefly, and he smiled that incandescent signature smile and I raised up as if I might levitate, both arms in the air, and I waved without restraint, an unabashed stadium wave, a come from behind, just before the buzzer, swish shot from mid-court wave.

The men in the black sedan, traveling close behind, regarded me coolly, appraisingly, and then the motorcade was gone.

What lingered and then grew from that day forward was my commitment to an idea that Kennedy had suggested for the first time on October 14, 1960, at the University of Michigan in Ann Arbor. A group of some 10,000 students had gathered, waiting into the earliest hours of the morning, to hear him speak. Kennedy began with some general remarks and then asked, "How many of you, who are going to be doctors, are willing to spend your days in Ghana? Technicians or engineers, how many of you are willing to work in the Foreign Service and spend your lives traveling around the world?"

Those words, reflecting a nascent idea, spoken in the early hours of a crisp Michigan morning, were expanded upon at the Cow Palace on November 2, 1960, just days before the election. Kennedy said, "Think of the wonders skilled American personnel could work, building goodwill, building peace. There is not enough money in all of America to relieve the misery of the underdeveloped world in a giant endless soup kitchen. But there is enough know-how and enough knowledgeable people to help those nations help themselves." It was then that he mentioned creating a Peace Corps of talented men and women, saying, "We cannot discontinue training our men as soldiers of war – but we also need them as ambassadors of peace."

With his election, that challenge, repeated again in his inaugural address – "Ask not what your country can do for you, ask what you can do for your country" – was soon transformed into the reality of the Peace Corps, a call to service that resonated with me and thousands of others who stepped forward, made a commitment that would take them to the remotest villages, the poorest towns, and the darkest urban slums of the world.

Even today I think of myself as a Kennedy volunteer. The Peace Corps will always possess his imprimatur. He called and we answered. We looked toward the horizon and said, in unison, send us. Let us do the work, live with the people. Their struggles will be our struggles. Their days will be our days. We can do this.

Of course, we didn't know anything about those distant places, not really. How could we? We came from the First World, from an inconceivable affluence. For some of us, the reality of the Third World was more than we could bear. For others, it was, at first, an experience to be endured. And then with time it brought an unexpected joy, an experience that was memorable beyond all years, life changing beyond all measure.

*   *   *

A small boy, naked from the waist down, stands in front of a tin roof shack, his face a smear of dirt. A ditch filled with a rancid mixture of sewage and garbage and foamy water borders his house.

His mother kneads cornmeal on a smooth board, dropping coarse flat cakes onto a blackened grill. Nearby is a plastic jug of water filled early that morning at a communal well, the barest hint of sunlight touching the horizon.

Gradually, with time, I came to understand that the stark, overwhelming, teeth-clenching contrasts between the First World and the Third World are not superficial but go to the bone. Life is lived on a precipice, an exhausting scramble for survival, filled with uncertainty and despair.

The images are haunting, ever-present.

No one has a lifestyle. Most will never have a career or go to college or possess a credit card. They will never walk through a mall or buy food by yelling into the mouth of a plastic clown or stand in an air-conditioned supermarket so filled with abundance as to be unimaginable. Few will ever enter a hospital of any kind, or turn on a faucet in a gleaming kitchen and watch potable water filling a glass, or open a refrigerator door and stand in the soft yellow glow contemplating the choices. They will never be bused from home to school or stand in line at a Starbucks or sit at a counter and order from a menu of indescribable choices or wander the shelves of a library.

The Third World can be a place so stark and foreign that it all but defies description. We peer, at first, through a distorted prism, and then, ever so slowly, we begin to see more clearly and come to understand and it is that understanding that changes everything forever.

AT FIRST LIGHT

Cartagena, Colombia, a city of colors and textures: the deep blue of the midday sky broken by massive billowing clouds; white buildings shaded by umbrella trees that cast long shadows across rococo balconies and narrow streets; the barrios a sprawl of sepia houses and dusty roads; the ocean on all sides a milky mix of cerulean and green.

Cartagena, a city of shimmering, sultry heat, the sun scorching the days, the air a tangible, gauzy curtain to be parted as a gentle rain falls in the late afternoon covering the streets and sidewalks with a steamy wet.

Many of the locals are black, meaning mocha and latte and terra brun, descended from slaves brought by Spain's colonists to labor in the fields and mines, to build huge coral revetments and fortresses along the mouth of the bay.

Surely it was those same people who built the ancient houses that surround a lovely plaza in the center of town where an ornate fountain sprays arching fantails of water into the air, marked by ethereal rainbows. Children often gather on the grass near the fountain and dance in the mist, their brown bodies glistening, their laughter breaking the midday stillness, their faces tilted upward, eyes shut, turning slowly with the joy of it.

The port, just outside the city walls, teems with life. Wooden boxes, filled with bananas and mangos, are stacked three or four deep. Fishing nets hang on listing poles, drying in the sun, and men sleep in colorful hammocks above the decks of fishing boats, shaded from the harsh afternoon sun by heavy canvas canopies. All is redolent of decaying fish and fruit and motor oil, mixed with an astringent, metallic odor that seems ever-present.

*   *   *

I had been in Cartagena only two days and already I was enchanted by its beauty, stunned by its poverty, finding it a place of startling and unsettling contrasts.

Early in the morning of my third day, eyes gritty, sleep elusive, I left the Plaza Hotel at first light and made my way along the narrow streets toward the ocean to a café I had noticed the day before. I carried a tattered copy of TIME Magazine under one arm and a paperback novel pushed down in my back pocket, my shields against a growing sense of isolation and loneliness.

The café was spacious, wood frame, painted green, its tin roof rust stained, canvas window coverings rolled up and tied. Inside were a few tables and chairs. A sign, yellow and green, hung above the doorway.

Entering, I noticed two women in the back, each wearing a light blue bib apron, ironing what looked to be white tablecloths. They both glanced up, their expressions curious. I sat at the table nearest the front, looking out at the empty street. It was still early and there were few people and little traffic. I listened to the muted sounds of the women ironing and talking, the irons hitting the cloth with muffled thuds, their words spoken softly.

I waited for a time, reading, anticipating strong coffee, warm bread, eggs mixed with onions and sausage. I was famished.

The morning light grew sharper, the sun now well above the horizon, already dominating the day. Across the street a dog came around a corner, moving slowly, pausing to stretch first one hind leg then the other, then walked stiffly over to a bush and sniffed. Finally, unsteadily, the dog lifted its hind leg.

Looking around the café, I noticed there were no menus, no napkins or flatware. But this was Colombia, and since I had arrived nothing had been as expected, nothing was as it seemed.

The day before, I had gone to a bank and stood in a line that wasn't a line but a cordial shoving match. I bought a few things at a small grocery store near the hotel and struggled to make myself understood when I asked for shaving cream. I couldn't think of the verb, *to shave*. An older woman, soon joined by her husband, stood behind the counter looking at me intently, curious, as I held up a make-believe can, squeezed white foam into my palm and mimicked shaving. Finally, the woman threw her hands up in the air, saying, "Sí! Sí! Jabón. Para afeitar su cara. El hombre quiere jabón." Soap to shave his face. The man wants shaving soap, she said, beaming at me.

6

Her husband raised both hands, "Jabón. Claro." Of course, soap. And he, too, shook an imaginary can, rubbing his hands together. "Jabón, para afeitar," he said smiling. "Jabón, sí," the woman said, nodding her head, seeming happy and relieved.

Encouraged, believing we were making progress, I said, "Sí, jabón. Afeitar. Tienen jabón?" Do you have soap?

The señora looked at me and smiled. "No. No jabón."

I passed the long afternoon sitting at a small table in an open-air café, surrounded by men in dark suits and narrow ties, many drinking rich black coffee in demitasse cups with water chasers, talking emphatically as the sun dropped toward the horizon. In the fading light I stared at a local newspaper, the headlines and paragraphs enigmatic, well beyond my countless hours of Spanish training.

That evening, in the hotel dining room, I ordered the catch of the day and was brought a plate of beef and tubular vegetables and the waiter stood next to me waiting until I took my first bite. When I did, he smiled at me and I smiled back, nodding my head in approval. Satisfied, he walked away toward the kitchen, a damp towel over his shoulder.

After my meal, I sat in the lobby of the hotel looking out at the park, a corner streetlamp casting a faint nimbus of light on the sidewalk, the fountain all but obscured. Feeling spent, I went up to my room and lay on the bed in the darkness watching the ceiling fan turn slowly, distant sounds reaching me. I tried to sleep.

* * *

Turning in my chair, I glanced back at the two women who were intent on their ironing, hoping to catch their eye, to say with my expression that I was ready to order. It would be the order I had practiced earlier, as I left my hotel: huevos rancheros, café y pan, por favor. I would say the words cleanly, clearly.

The two women continued to iron, one pushing her hair back behind her ears, occasionally dipping her hand in a tin of water, sprinkling the table cloth, water falling from her fingertips. The taller one looked across the room at me and said something to the other and they both glanced in my direction, smiling.

Putting down her iron on a raised metal plate, the taller one came to the front of the cafe and stood by my table. She was younger than I expected, her face flushed from the ironing. A long strand of deeply black hair clung to her damp forehead.

"Señor, qué quiere?" What do you want?

I answered in my best Spanish, delivering a wonderful order, offering it with great humility and politeness, my pronunciation cautious and precise. Feeling my confidence building, I asked for a favor: might she bring my coffee first.

A gringo who spoke Spanish and was mannerly. Already I was an ambassador of good will, ordering with ease and deference. I could do this.

The woman looked at me for a long moment, her eyes large and brown, absently touching her cheek with the back of her wrist. She wore a small gold cross on a delicate chain around her neck.

She turned and walked to the back, pausing near the other woman, and I heard them talking. They both looked in my direction and I smiled and they smiled in return. A faint, cooling breeze came off the ocean redolent of salt and drying seaweed, and just beyond the trees and buildings, in the distance, I could see a narrow stretch of beach and the Caribbean beyond. Scalloped fishnets hung on vertical poles, and a wooden dinghy lay on its side at the water's edge.

I pulled out my paperback, *Franny and Zooey,* and tried to read, waiting for the coffee.

After a time, the woman returned carrying a large porcelain cup of steaming coffee, setting it on the table first, then a plate of eggs and bread. In her apron pocket she had a knife and fork wrapped in a cloth napkin and a shaker of salt. She placed all in front of me and left.

The eggs were tender, the portion generous, the bread warm, the coffee strong and very good. People passed on the sidewalk, but no one entered the café and I sat alone at my table, taking my time with the meal, watching the street gradually fill with early morning traffic. On a corner, a man in a white tropical suit stood fanning himself with a folded newspaper, turning to look up at the sun. His suit was deeply creased at the arms and across his lap and his tie was already loosened.

Drinking the last of my coffee, I looked around for the women, but they were gone, the café empty. I waited and when they didn't appear, uncertain, I walked to the back, noticing piles of folded laundry stacked on a long wooden table, an old sewing machine, the name Singer written in ornate gold script, stood against one wall. Behind a curtain of beads I could make out a room with two narrow cots and in one corner a sink and pan for washing dishes. Spools of thread and remnants of material were piled neatly on a chair. "Señoras," I called out. No one answered.

Walking back to my table, I left thirty pesos under the coffee cup, hoping it was enough. Out on the street I looked back at the cafe and the sign above the door. *Vista Del Mar*. View of the Sea. Indeed.

I returned to my hotel and crossed the lobby. Already it was warm, the sun throwing shafts of bright light through the high, arching windows. The concierge, standing at the front desk, asked me if I had enjoyed my breakfast.

"Very well," I said. "The food was excellent and the coffee especially good."

"And where did you take your breakfast?" he asked, looking at me with interest.

"Just down the street. Near the ocean. The café with the yellow and green sign," I said, hesitating, searching for the Spanish word for sign.

"Yellow and green..." said the concierge. "Ah, yes. Did the sign say, 'Vista Del Mar'?"

"Sí. Sí, señor."

"Really. And you took your breakfast there?"

"Yes. A place very agreeable."

The concierge looked at me for a moment, then asked, "And who served you your breakfast?"

"A young woman, tall, one of two."

"Very good, señor," he said, a smile touching the corners of his mouth. "But before you return for another breakfast, you should know that this is a place where one takes one's laundry to be washed and ironed. The two women are the owners and they live in the back. They also sew and mend."

I stared at the concierge for a long moment, thinking back on the morning, the two women ironing, the meal brought to me, spools of thread and squares of folded cloth on the tables and chairs, and, of course, the sewing machine.

Over the concierge's shoulder I saw four old men sitting in large rattan chairs in the lobby, one reading a newspaper, holding it before him like a white sail, smoke from his cigar drifting above him, the others sipping coffee from small white cups, saying little, and in the park the fountain sent up a shimmering, luminescent spray carried by the wind up into the trees.

I looked at the concierge, weighing carefully what he had told me, finally saying, "That is a great shame, for I have never had a better cup of coffee."

THE NUNS

I had been stationed in Cartagena just long enough to fully realize it was the tropics. The sun was relentless, harsh, glaring, and I wouldn't have been surprised if late one afternoon it had simply refused to drop below the horizon.

Only in the early morning, briefly, all seemed fresh and cool, the breeze from the ocean reluctantly stirring the curtains of a small café where I ate breakfast most mornings.

I would soon start teaching at a local normal school. Until then, I looked for a room, perhaps in a residencia. Often, in the late afternoon, as the heat lifted, I wandered the streets of the city listening to the unfamiliar sounds, the hum of people and traffic, the language a type of Spanish I had never heard before, vowels and consonants swallowed, words offered in a staccato delivery, much of it unintelligible.

One Sunday morning I took a small ferry out to an island, just off shore. I had heard it was lush, lovely, encircled by clear blue waters.

And so it was. A postcard. Palm trees pushing down to crescent beaches, the interior a canopy of green against a washed-out sky.

The ferry moored at a long, narrow dock and I stood for a moment, taking it all in. Cabanas, each with an abbreviated porch, painted a riot of bright colors, red and yellow and blue, were pushed back, beneath sheltering palm trees.

A tienda, a small store, was just off to the left, one corner sinking into the sand, the corrugated tin roof covered with dried palm leaves. Tables and chairs were bunched near the front like an afterthought, and ragged yellow and blue umbrellas stood at odd angles, creating fragments of shade.

At the tienda I bought two rolled tortillas filled with chicken, cradled in wax paper, and a cold beer. For a time I sat under an umbrella, on a chair fashioned from a tin drum, and watched the ferry gently rise and fall, the mooring lines never coming into play. The tortillas were sublime, salsa dripping down my chin, the beer, straight from the bottle, so cold my eyes watered.

Then, as so often happened during those first weeks, despite the surrounding beauty, I was overwhelmed by a sense of isolation. Great good God, I thought, why am I here?

As I gazed north, my eyes lingered on the horizon, the blue water stretching in all directions. North meant home. America. California. And all that was familiar and known and predictable and oh-so-easy.

So easy. What was I thinking? John Kennedy, who lived in the White House and had room service, called for volunteers, challenging them to ask what they could do for their country: be of service, live in a Third World country, dig a well, stand in front of a class of eager students, point the way.

And guess who had raised his hand? Yours truly. It wasn't Kennedy sitting on a tin drum on an atoll in the middle of the ocean five thousand miles from a Laundromat. Hadn't someone, in a lucid moment, pointed out that you should never volunteer? Isn't that written somewhere? You, the one with your hand up, the one wearing rose-colored granny glasses, idealism etched in your naive smile: Please. Quickly. Put your hand down. Unless, of course, you have an affinity for places so remote and strange that the world, your world, suddenly seems a dream.

I walked from the tienda along the shoreline, coming around a promontory to a small sheltered cove revealing a slip of white sand shaded by a necklace of palm trees. The waves barely crested as they gently rolled toward the beach.

I sat leaning against a palm tree, watching small brown seabirds run through the foamy surf on long, fragile legs, their spade-like beaks probing the wet sand for small creatures. The wind moved the heavy palms above me, a whisper of dry paper, and birds chattered in the dense brush. Otherwise, all was quiet.

Not only had I volunteered, I prayed to whatever God was listening that I would get through the training, learn the language, and survive the physical challenges. Countless hours of Spanish – conjugation of verbs, endless vocabulary, halting conversations in present and future tenses. And the phys ed coaches. They were fanatics, Mach 1 jocks with their hair on fire, planning, with satisfied grins, forced marches through the Sangre De Cristo Mountains of New Mexico, Outward Bound the steely template. And each evening, feeling cold and bone tired, we brewed a gumbo of dried meat and potatoes, boiled in a soot-covered pot over the coals of a small fire, seasoned with a litany of platitudes resembling mantras: "What doesn't kill you only makes you stronger." Followed by a chuckle, a grin, then, "Of course, first we try to kill you."

And those purveyors of the crucible of character, who worshipped at the shrine of hustle, our coaches, our instructors, reported back to the staff shrinks, the high priests of "normal," describing every nuance of our behavior, every tic, every slouching, grouchy, exhausted moment, made credible by their weighty specificity.

And to our surprise, our joy, how sweet and unexpected, after months of training, we were handed passports, immunization cards, folding money, and flown as a group to Bogotá, Colombia, where we would be assigned our in-country domiciles.

Touching down in Colombia, an electric, palpable sense of anticipation, even euphoria, gripped us. Soon we were shuttled to a large downtown hotel and assigned rooms. A few of us stood in a tiled bathroom, commenting that there were two toilets, one, we were told, a bidet that shot water straight up like a small geyser at Yellowstone Park. I stood at the white enamel sink looking suspiciously at the spigot, wondering what manner of small parasites might be hiding in the water.

We had arrived and spent a week in host country meetings, lectures from the medical staff, the embassy staff, later exchanging our passports for visas of a sort that explained we were with the U.S. government. Most evenings, at twilight, we walked the wide and busy avenidas of Bogotá. We had arrived.

And weeks later, in Cartagena, I still didn't have a clue where to get anything washed, or where the buses went, or what words I might patch together like some randomly stitched quilt, even remotely resembling a request for directions.

And not to forget that long night spent sitting on a bidet, vomiting into the toilet. The culprit? Maybe the chicken-on-a-stick, bought for five pesos from a street vendor, happily sautéed in a kitchen no health department would ever see. And wiping his hands on a limp hand towel, once white, now the color of tobacco, the vendor, flashing gold-capped teeth, took my crumpled bills, smiled politely, perhaps sympathetically, and watched curiously as I walked away.

13

Dear God. My kingdom for a pop tart. A burger. A no-worries drink of water straight from the tap. A bag of day-old fries. A glass of oh-so-cold milk, homogenized. Anything ordered from a laminated menu while seated on a swivel chair of bright chrome and red vinyl, delivered with a smile by a waitress named Flo who offers just one word, "enjoy," in a husky, cigarette voice, a voice so familiar, so friendly, that just the thought of it, even now, brings tears to my eyes.

Sighing deeply, I gazed absently along the beach, and suddenly, coming around the point, walking on the firm, wet sand was a black man leading six nuns, each in full habit. Their robes, heavy and flowing, covering them completely, were a startling, brilliant white, their faces framed by arched veils, making it difficult to see their expressions. All walked with hands hidden in cavernous sleeves, large black crosses swinging at their waists.

They moved in a tentative line, close behind the black man, who stopped at the water's edge. He wore khaki shorts and a faded red shirt, buttoned only at the bottom. Smiling and nodding, he motioned for the nuns to come close.

I sat very still, captivated, their presence on the beach so unexpected, so improbable, that all I could do was watch in wonder. The man spoke to them, his voice lost in the wind. But I could see his white teeth flashing, his gestures emphatic and animated.

Abruptly, without hesitation, the nuns began to slip off their shoes and long black stockings, helping each other to balance. The man nodded in encouragement and waded out into the water, leaving a line of wet on his shorts. Turning back, he gestured to them, laughing, dipping his cupped hands into the water and then lifting them up, letting the water spill over his face and slide down his arms, calling to them, "Vengan." Come. See how wonderful it is.

As if by common agreement, the nuns walked toward him, their arms lifted high in the air, the ocean swirling around them. Some clapped their hands, and I could see their smiles, hear their laughter, their robes flaring about them, ballooning with each wave like enormous white jellyfish.

The man came out of the water and took the hand of a nun who had ventured in only far enough to wet the hem of her robe. He pulled and coaxed her until she was standing up to her waist in the undulating swells. I heard her call out in surprise and delight, splashing the water with the flat of her hands, turning slowly like some strange, pirouetting ballerina.

In that one magical moment, a leitmotif for the weeks and months that would follow, my isolation and wrenching loneliness fell away, forgotten. There was only the beach and the nuns and the black man.

Watching them was poetic and lovely and I sat and stared, wanting never to forget the tableau before me: those remarkable nuns, moving in graceful slow motion, their white robes swirling, merging, framed by the glorious blue water.

THE HOTEL

On a finger of land, a narrow peninsula called Bocagrande, stands a three-story hotel named El Caribe. Stunningly white, shaded by lush evergreen trees, it faces out to the ocean. Rattan lounge chairs, umbrellas and round glass tables surround a pristine pool.

For a time, while I waited for my assignment to begin, the Caribe was my sanctuary. I had rented a room in an aging residencia downtown and I often woke early, before first light, and lay very still listening to the street sounds. Getting up, I would stand looking out the window into the shadows of the approaching dawn. And then, as the sky turned a mottled, pinkish blue, I dressed and left the residencia and took the bus out to the hotel.

Walking between the white stucco pillars, each covered with climbing bougainvillea, the delicate flowers purple and red and white, I made my way up a long driveway bordered by dense fronds and orange and red hibiscus. A chorus of birds chattered in the tall trees, the sun, already warm, filtering through the umbrella of leaves.

During those first weeks, I often spent the morning sitting by the pool, at a table shaded by an umbrella, sipping coffee, struggling to read the local paper, finally giving up and retreating to a paperback novel, one of more than 100 that sat near my bed in a battered Peace Corps book locker, a locker that had been passed along to me by another volunteer. Every one had been read hard, the covers ragged, the spines broken.

The smatterings of conversations from the nearby tables were international, German and French and Portuguese, and, of course, Spanish. The people seemed exotic and I wondered how they came to be at the Caribe, of all places. For a time, an older man sat with two young women, both lovely, their hair long and brown, their smooth skin deeply tanned, speaking what I assumed was Portuguese. On one occasion, the man came to the table from the beach, slipping on an elegant guayabera shirt, and I noticed several raised scars on his chest the size of quarters, the skin a shiny, speckled white. Whenever I saw the three of them together, no matter the early hour, they talked amiably, laughed, and the girls had wide, charming smiles, their teeth white and even. Was he a general who had escaped Germany after World War II with a suitcase of gold bars or several paintings that should now be hanging in the Louvre, sold for a fortune to buy a massive cattle ranch in the remotest part of Brazil? I wanted desperately to know who they were, their histories, how this odd threesome came to be. Were the women his daughters, his consorts, his paid companions? I never found out. One morning the table was empty, set for breakfast but no one came to sit or talk or laugh as the sun rose above the palm trees and the roofline of the hotel.

Later, after breakfast, I went down to the beach and sat for a time, and then I swam out, floating in the tepid Caribbean, looking at the shore, the outline of the hotel, people walking in the sudsy whitewater as the gentle waves broke on the beach and swirled around their ankles. There was an outdoor shower where I rinsed off, the water cold and refreshing. At midday I left the hotel and walked back between the pillars, and stood waiting for the bus, the balmy trade winds rustling high in the trees.

* * *

I soon realized that my clothes needed to be washed, my shirts stiff from sweat and repeated wear. Chagrined, I returned to the laundry not far from the beach, to the wood frame house with the slats a faded green, the tin roof streaked with rust. The Vista Del Mar.

Some weeks before, the Plaza Hotel concierge had explained to me that the owner was a Señora Consuelo Cruz. She lived in the back with her niece, Pilar. Señora Cruz was a short, stocky woman, her hair streaked with gray, her smile startling because of gold caps on her front teeth. Pilar was taller, more angular, very quiet and a student at an all girls' colegio, not far from the laundry.

They had not seen me since that early morning breakfast, and now I stood in the doorway with an armload of laundry. Both stopped ironing and looked at me and waited.

I gestured with my sack of clothes and said, "Señora, señorita, I've returned. But… not for a meal. My clothes… they need washing."

I thought they might laugh, but instead they told me to enter, that indeed I had come to the right place, this time, and I should bring my sack to the back of the laundry and put it on a table. The señora asked my name and wrote it carefully in an old ledger. "Bueno," she said. "Your clothes will be ready in a week."

And so it began.

Whenever I returned, I often found señora Cruz standing at a long table, pushing a heavy chrome iron over damp sheets or white shirts, which she carefully folded and placed into deep wicker baskets nearby. Some mornings, before the heat of the day took hold, she sat hunched over her black Singer sewing machine, mending shirts and sheets. Faintly, in the background, I heard salsa music from an ancient black radio that sat on a shelf along with soaps and bleaches and tin measuring cups.

All of the windows were open, the canvas coverings rolled up, and trade winds gently passed through, and on still days, when the heat seemed enveloping, a fan in the ceiling turned slowly with a creaking, uneven sway.

The señora did indeed wash my clothes, and I soon learned that it wasn't so much washing as committing assault and battery on my cotton shirts and pants. With a single-minded intensity, she scrubbed my shirts on a flat stone, angled over a much-used tub filled with soapy water. Over time the collars and cuffs began to fray, the material distressed. It was then that she reversed them, working expertly on the sewing machine, pushing the treadle slowly, up and down.

Whenever I arrived to pick up my laundry, she stopped what she was doing and insisted that I sit near the front of the store, at one of the wooden tables. She brought out a tray with heavy porcelain cups filled with steaming coffee and we sat together, drinking the coffee, looking out at the passing traffic and the people walking past and the blue water beyond.

At first she asked me questions about my time in Cartagena, knowing that my first weeks had been difficult. "Why would your mother permit you to come to a place so far away from your home, to live in Cartagena?" she asked, smiling. "And what is this thing you call El Cuerpo de Paz?"

She always spoke slowly, knowing that I had to grapple with the words and the sentences. And if I didn't grasp every word, she waited, confident that I understood the meaning and intention of her questions.

I explained that the Peace Corps – el Cuerpo de Paz, the Body of Peace – was an agency of the United States government. I would soon begin teaching in a colegio where young women prepared to teach children in the elementary schools, some in the barrios surrounding Cartagena, others in the nearby countryside.

Señora Cruz listened politely and asked, "But why do you come here?" She said this kindly, her curiosity genuine, her intelligence obvious, and I knew that it was a relevant, probing question. I constructed a short answer having to do with wanting to help other people – volunteers dug wells, taught health classes, and worked in schools.

But I knew that her question was larger than my capacity to answer. It would take time before I would have it sorted out.

Gradually I came to understand that the volunteers weren't in Colombia to change the country. We had come to do small things, seemingly insignificant things, things of no real consequence when viewed in a context of decades and even centuries.

In the exchange of information and in the quality of our interactions, in the process of constructing a small schoolhouse, in planting a straight row of corn or discussing health issues with a group of women, we came to know one another and soon recognized our common humanity.

The locals understood that we were not passing through with cameras and guide maps. Instead we hunkered down. We had come to stay, to share in the rhythms of their lives and share those of our own. We set out to learn the language and the customs while submerging ourselves in the culture, out of respect and appreciation and sometimes wonder.

Anything less would have been hubris, a remnant of the colonial syndrome blatantly perpetuated in the past by countless nations wherein white men and women arrived and with a sense of unchallenged superiority, absent any invitation or understanding, set about offering a seductive aid accompanied by their values or religion. It's a trap that those from the First World fall into repeatedly, no matter what history or experience has taught.

I didn't understand it then, not at first, but I wish I had, for I could have shared it with señora Cruz and I think she would have understood.

* * *

Early one morning, the day still cool, the bus dropped me at the entrance to the Caribe. Next to one of the pillars stood a man on crutches, his left leg missing below the knee, his empty pant leg folded up and tied off with soiled string. I had never seen him before.

Watching me approach, he banged a large tin cup on the side of the pillar, the sound sharp and emphatic. My first reaction was to quickly walk past, eyes averted, feeling intimidated by his need and the depths of his poverty. With one glance I knew that he lived in an abyss of struggle and pain and anger and humiliation.

On impulse I slowed and took a five-peso note and walked over to him. I thought he would hold out the cup so I could place the money inside. But he didn't. Instead he stared at me out of one eye. I saw that the other eye was a milky gray, covered by an impenetrable cataract.

"Why do you take the bus?" he asked. "You are a rich gringo, no?"

"No," I said. "I'm not rich."

He shifted on his crutches. He was wearing a white shirt, soiled and stiff, the collar frayed, the elbows torn, his long hair matted and wild, his face a burnt sienna, deeply lined, sparse strands of beard barely concealing his jaw line. His hands were gnarled, the nails blackened and broken.

Again I held out the five pesos and waited, my body leaning toward the entryway signaling that I was leaving.

Still he held back the cup and looked at me closely. "So, who are you, gringo, if you are not rich? Tell me."

Suddenly curious about this man and his unwillingness to quietly accept the offered bill, I took a step back in his direction.

I began to answer him and stopped. There was nothing I could say or do that would change anything, and the idea that there was just six degrees of separation between us was sheer myth. We peered at each other across a chasm of experience. I could no more change his life than he could change mine.

I looked at the man and took the bill and offered it to him and not his cup. "Aquí. Por favor," I said. Here. Please. Placing the note in the pocket of his shirt I walked through the pillars and up the long driveway toward the hotel.

When I left later that morning he was gone. I did see him one afternoon, standing on a downtown street, staring forward, people moving around him as if he were a rock in a stream, his cup hanging from a string around his neck.

Over the next weeks and months I sought the man out, on a street corner, in a narrow alley, near a bus stop, and often, before I saw him, I would hear the banging of his tin cup. I always gave him five pesos and he would say, "Pues, gringo, qué pasa?" What's happening? And little else. We would look at one another and I asked him how he was and he nodded, saying, "Como siempre." As always. And then I would walk away toward my residencia, the sound of his tin cup banging on his crutch, brittle and mournful.

A PLACE APART

For weeks Cartagena had simmered, smelling of decaying fish and overripe mangos, fanned by vagrant breezes from the Caribbean that barely stirred the trees and never brought relief.

Walking home late one Sunday afternoon, the sun low in the sky, I saw Paco sitting at a table in an outdoor café sipping beer, reading a local paper.

Paco had been in Colombia as a volunteer for almost two years and moved at a pace decidedly slower than my own. His shirt worn, his khakis washed almost white, everything about him seemed faded, remote, his conversation always laconic, often sliding into cynicism.

Seeing me he smiled, saying, "Pues hombre, qué pasa?"

The café was one of my favorites, the spreading trees providing ample shade, the ocean just a stretch of beach away. I sat down with a beer I'd bought at the bar.

"Paco, how goes it?"

"Poco a poco, lad." Little by little.

His beer bottle in one hand, his elbows resting on the arms of his chair, Paco looked out at the ocean. I picked up a section of his paper and tried to make sense out of the news, and finally leaned back, watching the people, the ebb and flow of traffic, still trying to absorb where I was and the meaning of it all.

A bus passed, a rainbow of yellow, blue, and red, filled beyond capacity, a flashing Madonna in the window. An old man, white hair, a full beard, stood in the open door of the bus, one hand grasping a vertical chrome bar, the other pressing a package tightly against his chest. He stared at me with sad, rheumy eyes. Women, wearing diaphanous cotton dresses, small children in hand, walked by carrying fishnet shopping bags filled with fruits and vegetables and small items wrapped in brown paper, their faces damp from the heat.

A beggar at the corner sat on a square of ragged plywood with metal wheels, his emaciated legs tucked under him, a wooden bowl wedged between his thighs. His desolate face said he knew he was invisible and nothing he did, no entreaty to those who passed by, not even the banging of his bowl on the sidewalk, would ever make him real. I looked away.

Since my arrival I had felt slightly off balance and often found myself staring into the distance, seeing but not seeing.

Paco pushed back from the table and stood up, saying, "Gotta roll, chief." He paused, looking down at me. "Tell you what, why don't you come along, there's a place I want to show you."

He crossed the street and I followed. We walked together, sunlight spilling around us, lush palmettos bordering the sidewalk. He told me that he was due to return stateside in a couple of weeks and wasn't sure how he felt about leaving.

"Believe it or not – and I'd say right now, for you, it's not – this place grows on you." He said this with a knowing smile and a nod of his head. "Trust me."

Abruptly he turned, heading down a narrow path and through an arched opening in a high coral stone wall, shards of glass set in mortar on top, vines of red and white bougainvillea crawling up the side. We stepped into a room the size of a large pantry. On the opposite wall was a narrow, smoked-glass window fixed on a metal track, allowing it to slide open. Just below, on an abbreviated shelf, was a small, silver bell.

Paco walked over and picked up the bell and shook it several times, the brittle sound filling the room. I watched and waited, wondering if I was about to witness Paco's confession. After a moment, the window slid open and I caught a glimpse of a hand placing a small brown paper bag on the shelf, then withdrawing, the window closing with a firm thud.

Paco took the bag and walked past me, his forefinger to his lips, cautioning me not to speak. We returned to the cafe, to the table we had occupied earlier, our empty beer bottles and newspaper where we had left them.

Sitting down I looked at Paco and at the bag, finally saying, "What?"

"That was a nunnery. All the sisters and the novitiates who live there are cloistered. They never leave. Have no contact with the outside world.

Every Sunday morning they take Holy Communion, and in the afternoon they put the leftover communion bread in these small sacks and hand them through the window to whoever rings the bell."

I looked back in the direction we had come, thinking of the high vine-covered walls, the broken glass on top, and tried to comprehend a group of women living out their lives in a place completely apart.

I imagined that behind the walls were large wooden doors with ornate locks and courtyards with discrete gardens, austere cubicles for sleeping, a chapel diminished by an enormous cross, nuns walking in silence along dim corridors, heads bowed, hands hidden in the sleeves of their ample robes, sublimely reverent and always penitent.

They took their meals in a great room, sitting at rough hewn tables, eating from chipped porcelain bowls, the silence broken only by the muted sounds of dishes being moved and passed along, or water being poured into heavy enamel cups. Theirs was a life defined by an ongoing dialogue with God, words of abiding belief offered up as whispered prayers, all the while patiently waiting, listening intently for a reply. I could not begin to understand such a choice.

Paco opened the bag and handed me a wedge of wafer-like bread, delicate, a pale creamy white. Chewing slowly, he said, "The deal is this. The hand you saw, the one that passed the sack through the opening, it's always the same one. Without fail. See, I think it's the hand of a novitiate, a girl who hasn't taken her final vows. Meaning, she's not a real nun. At least not yet."

"How can you tell?" I asked.

"If she were a total nun, she'd be wearing a ring. No ring, no vows. You're still in the minors."

Paco said this leaning back in his chair, taking another wafer and placing it carefully on the flat of his tongue, gazing abstractly down the street toward the nunnery.

I knew Paco had been in Colombia for a full tour. But sitting there, looking at him, listening to his description of the novitiate's hand, I wondered if perhaps he hadn't stayed too long. I'd heard he lived alone, had a small room in back of a large stone house near the ocean. He taught arithmetic and coached soccer at a small elementary school and wandered the streets of Cartagena late into the night, seeking refuge in obscure bars, often spending time with locals, men in soiled, deeply wrinkled linen suits, and women in garish satin dresses stretched tightly across their round abdomens.

Paco, holding his empty beer bottle in front of him on the table, pushing absently at one corner of the damp label with his thumbnail, looked up, saying, "Deal is, I'm heading back to the states shortly. And the one thing I want to do before I leave is see that novitiate. Just a look, no more. Otherwise, I'm going to spend the rest of my life wondering about her."

I looked at Paco incredulously. "You're serious? I mean, all I saw was a flash of white hand before the window slid home."

"Yeah, I know. But I've been going there a long time. Picking up communion wafers. Standing in that small room, waiting for the window to slide back. Sometimes her hand lingers. Happens when I'm alone. Like she's not sure she wants to close the window. You know what it's like when you spot an incredible girl, maybe you're walking along the street or in a department store or sitting in a restaurant and there she is and there's something about her, the way she smiles, her hair, her eyes, and your heart gives a jump, and you can't stop looking at her or trying to figure out how you might meet her. That's what it's like every time I see the novitiate's hand."

"Damn, Paco. That's a cloister. Those ladies are locked away. What're the odds you could get even a quick look?"

Paco walked over to the bar and leaned on the counter. He raised two fingers and the bartender put two longneck beers in front of him, white foam spilling down the sides. Paco gave the man some crumpled bills and returned to our table, handing me one of the bottles.

Saying thanks, I placed a wafer on my tongue, chewed slowly, then raised my beer giving him a salud. "Here's to novitiates, wherever they may be."

Paco smiled, drinking deeply. "Well, I know where one is. And that would be the one I have to see. Question is, how? I've thought of passing her a note. Maybe push a folded piece of paper through the opening before the window closes. Say something like, 'Señorita, por favor, no cierra la ventana.' Get her to wait, and not close the window. All I need is a moment."

Paco looked off into the distance, moving his beer back and forth between his hands, and took a deep breath.

"But nothing sounds right," he said. "Hell, I've actually considered ringing the bell and then running back outside, climbing up on the wall, wait for her to appear on the other side. Anything to see her face. Pretty amazing when you think about it. I've done all this community development, taught little kids math, dug trenches, put on roofs, given health talks. And when the time comes to leave, all I can think about is that one incredible hand. Belonging to a novitiate, no less, who is not yet the bride of Christ. Not yet, lad. Kills me to leave without meeting her. I think I'm in love."

Paco shook his head, glancing over at me as if his own words had caught him completely by surprise. "You believe this?" he said, more to himself than to me. "Man, I've definitely been here too long. I've heard it happens to some volunteers. They go native, lose themselves, maybe a part of their mind. Get twitchy and strange. I don't know, man."

For a time we sat in silence, both of us thinking about the novitiate. "Paco, look, there's no way. Not a chance you'll get within ten feet of her. Least of all actually talk to her. I mean, I've heard that you can barely date the local girls, the ones on *this* side of the wall. And if you do, you have three aunts and a grandmother with you, and that's after you've taken a vow of celibacy administered by the girl's father."

In truth, the local families guarded their daughters with a phalanx of older women in black stockings and shawls, professional chaperones all, alert for any false move toward their adorable charges. And being a gringo didn't help. Hollywood had cemented our reputations and the abuelas, the grandmothers, knew our intentions long before we did. So while the young women of Colombia presented a weighty challenge, I assumed that novitiates, well, they would be the Everest of dating, existing at an altitude well beyond our reach.

Paco took another wafer between forefinger and thumb and studied it before putting it on his tongue, chasing it with a long swallow of beer. "That's a fact, amigo. Getting to first base with the local darlings... even a seat in the ballpark... well, better men have tried. So, seeing her would definitely be a challenge, her long black hair, lips the color of plums, eyes brown and innocent, a smile that would stop traffic. Damn."

Paco shifted in his chair and looked at me for a moment, saying, "But you know what also makes me a little crazy? It's the idea that that sweet novitiate will never leave the nunnery. Think about it, hidden away inside, cloistered all of her life. She'll never take a walk down a street alone in the early morning, see the sun breaking above the horizon. Never slow-dance to Johnny Mathis or Ray Charles. Never sit in a car with someone late at night, looking up at the stars, talking about nothing important. Or wake up in the dark of midnight, wondering what really happened to JFK. How about sitting at the counter in some drive-in, digging into an obscenely large cheeseburger, fries, a shake so thick the straw stands straight up in the glass while the juke box plays Elvis singing *That's All Right Mama* and you can't keep your legs from moving. Or walk along the ocean, where the sand is all wet and firm, white water swirling around your ankles, the smell of damp seaweed mixed up with the salt air. Sit in a park and listen to the voices of kids. Ride a roller coaster. See a movie. Drop from a rope into the cool water of a swimming hole. All the good stuff in life, and there's so much good stuff. Think about it."

For a long moment I stared off into the distance, contemplating Paco's litany of things missed, my lips pressed together in a thin line. "I have, Paco. Trust me. I've thought about it. And I can think of a hundred things and more without even trying. Truth is, the minute I got to Colombia I started on a list and it sure as hell isn't getting any shorter."

"Give it time, amigo. Give it time. Year from now, you won't even remember what was on it. You'll have a new one, much more local. May even have your own novitiate on it."

We left the café just as the sun slipped below the horizon, the light a soft yellow glow surrounding us. I glanced back toward the nunnery, thinking of the smoked-glass window, the alabaster hand holding the small paper sack of wafers.

I didn't see Paco before he left Cartagena and so never heard if he ever saw his novitiate. I was told there had been a small farewell party for him at a bar down by the docks, more ad hoc than anything else, mostly locals and some fishermen who happened to be sitting at a nearby table and were happy to join in. And then he was gone.

One Sunday afternoon, some weeks later, feeling restless and at loose ends, I returned to the nunnery, passing through the opening in the wall, standing in the small somber room looking at the window, an inexplicable excitement gripping me. After a moment, I rang the bell, waiting, hoping.

But the hand that slid the paper bag through the opening was old, mottled, the long fingers gnarled. Where was she? I wondered. Had she seen Paco? Had he shaken her faith? Was she now, this minute, out in the world?

I never returned to the nunnery, though I often thought of the novitiate. Like Paco, I knew she was splendid. Her large brown eyes framed by compassion, her lush femininity concealed by heavy robes, her long plaited hair gathered up beneath the delicate wimple of her habit. A beauty barely contained. How could it be otherwise?

And then I thought of her commitment and her faith and I thought of my own. Out here, out in the all of it.

THE BOOK LOCKER

Ticket in hand, I stood outside the Bogotá station looking at the buses. They were massive, garish, a mix of red and blue and orange. On the dashboards were plastic Madonnas, heads bowed, hands pressed together in prayer.

The bus ride to San Antonio, a small town in the Andes, would take the better part of the day and I didn't relish the journey.

Brassy music played loudly in the distance and I watched one bus pull away, filled to capacity, the brakes letting out a whoosh of air before rolling slowly down the street, the brake lights blinking brightly. A child, his face pressed against the back window, stared out at me with large, dark eyes.

Men in worn suit jackets and khaki pants, with sacks and satchels, women in cotton dresses carrying fishnet bags and parcels wrapped in stiff paper, some with small children, stood waiting for a bus to Medellín, a city hours away.

Spotting a bus that said San Antonio, I boarded, giving up my ticket, and with my duffle in hand walked to the back.

Dust seeped up through the worn floorboards, the air pungent with the smell of diesel gasoline and people and bags of food. One old man sat very still, holding a basket of eggs on his lap.

The buses of Colombia were infamous, the stuff of urban legend among Peace Corps Volunteers, and their drivers, well, they were feared, not for their size – most were no larger than jockeys – but for their pedal-to-the-metal abandon. They were strutting matadors who dared the bulls, embraced blind curves, horns blaring, powered onto soft shoulders, deep ravines mere inches away, all the while talking absently with the jefe segundo whose sole job was to open and close the bifurcated door using a chrome handle.

Though I had been in-country several months, I still found myself thinking of home. Sometimes, in irrational moments, I worried that California, even America, would not be there when I returned. Or would be changed. Not as I had left it. How many times had I inventoried every large and small thing I had taken for granted, everything I loved and now missed beyond words. I even started to write things down on the last blank page of whatever paperback book I was reading. Some of the items were strangely shallow, of no consequence: I wanted a chocolate malt in a glass that was perspiring from the cold and left a ring of damp on the napkin, a malt thick and rich with a small mound of whipped cream on top and with the first wonderful sip my nose would ache in this kind of wonderful way.

Of course, I missed refrigerators and televisions and my old Chevy, with the blown-out upholstery, and supermarkets and malls. And I missed my parents. There was the heart-wrenching thought of walking into our living room and seeing my parents sitting there, as I had countless times before, my mom on the sofa and my dad in his recliner, and feeling inexplicably reassured and happy.

The day before leaving for San Antonio, wanting to hear their voices, I went to a public exchange to call. A sign over the entry said Teléfono Publico, and it looked like a bus station with wide, unwashed windows and high, beveled glass doors. Inside was a large room, expansive, the floor a worn green linoleum. Two clerks sat behind ornate metal bars, writing down phone numbers and taking pesos for each call.

I stood in line, waiting my turn. The clerk was an older woman with salt-and-pepper hair and a shadow of mustache. She asked for my number. I told her, in my rehearsed Spanish, that I wanted to call the United States. "Los Estados Unidos," I said. "California." And I handed her the number, written on a slip of gray paper. She looked first at the paper and then at me. She had gold studs in her ears and a delicate lace handkerchief pinned on a demure gray dress. She opened a book and ran her forefinger down a row of locations and prices. "Sesenta pesos," she said. Sixty. Her eyes told me that to pay such a great amount was to abandon all common sense.

I counted out the bills.

"Bueno," she said, and told me that she would call my name and I was to go to booth 8. She gestured toward a wall of wooden booths, each with a number on top.

"Gracias," I said.

I sat on a long slatted bench to wait, at first watching people come and go. A few men were reading newspapers, some smoking short cigars, a woman whispered admonishments to her restless children.

I always carried a paperback and I tried to read. It was Steinbeck's *Cannery Row,* and I was captivated by the characters and longed to be on the Monterey coast, fingers of fog lifting as the sun warmed the day, the cool air touched by smells of salt water and pine trees.

I then thought of the many lazy afternoons I had spent on the deck at Sam's Restaurant in Tiburon, looking out at Angel Island and at the green waters of Raccoon Strait, sailboats in relief against the shoreline, and enormous ships slipping under the Golden Gate, their decks stacked high with cargo

I heard my name called and I glanced over at the woman, who nodded and pointed toward booth 8. I stepped inside, pulled the door closed, and picked up a heavy black phone.

"Hello?" I said. "Hello?" Nothing. Only the hiss of the line. "Hello?"

I heard a thin, distant voice say, "Hello."

"Hello? Dad? Is that you?" A crackling hiss came in return. "Hello? Hello?"

I felt suddenly angry, overwhelmed, tired of searching for every word in Spanish, tired of asking for directions, tired of ordering one kind of food and getting another, tired of feeling continually, maddeningly off balance. The deep frustration brought tears to my eyes as I began yelling into the phone, "Dad? Can you hear me, dad? Hello?" Nothing. Only a flat hum, broken by static.

I hung up the phone and stood there for a moment, looking at the black box, at the dull plastic phone and thin cord. I turned, pushing the door open, and emerged from the booth. The room seemed unusually quiet and I glanced at the clerk who had helped me. She raised her hand, gesturing that I should return to her window, but I couldn't bear to hear her explanation or, I imagined, having her return my pesos with a shake of her head. *Gringos. How strange they are.* I was certain that the children stared at me in wonder and the men peered at me over the tops of their newspapers, momentarily interested. I simply left, and walked out through the doors and into the midday heat. Breathe, I told myself. Remember to breathe.

The bus arrived in San Antonio late in the afternoon. The kamikaze wheel jockey had not killed us. Though he tried. I had come to visit Jim, a volunteer who was leaving Colombia shortly. He had given me his address and directions to his flat over a cantina. There was some talk that I might replace him.

I walked from the bus station and crossed a wide plaza of stone and brown tufts of grass, a waterless fountain in the center. The church, its square steeple topped with a cross, wide doors open to a dark interior, bordered the plaza. To the left was the casa corral, a white, flat building with a terra cotta tile roof, home to the local priest.

I stopped an old man and asked him if he could tell me where the Cantina Azul was, the Blue Cantina. He smiled, his teeth the color of dried tobacco. A white rectangle of cloth was folded over his right shoulder and a long machete hung from his belt. He nodded, saying, "Sí. Sí, señor," and he pointed to a corner across the plaza. "Allí." There. "La Cantina."

I thanked him and, with my duffel in hand, I walked past the fountain. I was struck by the quiet and the absence of people. A dog barked in the distance and two small boys ran across the plaza, kicking a ball. A woman stood in a doorway folding a towel, and then reached down and picked up a watering can and went back inside. Small red flowers grew in a lone pot on the narrow stoop.

A nun, her habit a startling white, left the casa corral and walked up the steps of the church, her face obscured, her hands concealed in the full sleeves of her robe. She never glanced in my direction. A campesino leading a donkey removed his straw hat as she passed, holding it against his chest.

Standing on the landing I knocked on Jim's door, hoping he was in. I could hear music from the cantina below. The well of the stairs smelled of fried food and stale beer and cigarette smoke. People were laughing, their voices loud, then falling away into silence.

The door opened. "Hey, Jaime," I said, using his Spanish name.

"Hola, Cristobal," he said. "You made it. Nice bus ride, huh." It wasn't a question, but an understanding of what was involved.

"Quite a ride. Only passed on curves, never on straight-aways. Other than that, poco a poco," I said.

I looked around his flat – narrow bed pushed against one wall, a wooden table and two chairs, the bathroom with a sink, the shower a spigot sticking out of a concrete wall, the water always cold.

His clothes hung on pegs on the wall. In one corner sat a Peace Corps book locker, filled with paperbacks, and books were stacked on the table, next to a writing pad and an empty beer bottle with a candle pushed down into the opening. Electricity was iffy, he said.

Jim went into the bathroom and from the toilet tank took two beers, dripping water on the unfinished wooden floor. We sat until darkness filled the windows and the sounds of the cantina below grew louder, raspy music mingling with voices and laughter. He talked of his two years in San Antonio, of his friendship with the padre, of the many meals that they had shared across a table in the casa corral and of his long rides back country.

I told him of walking through downtown Bogotá not long ago with a fellow volunteer, Ted, who just arrived. He was distracted and uncertain about his assignment and about remaining in Colombia. We stepped into the street and a car pulled in front of us, narrowly missing Ted, and stopped, waiting for the light to change. Ted stood there, looking at the dark sedan and the driver, then crawled up on the hood and slid over the other side. The driver was first astonished, then outraged. He jumped from the car, yelling a string of Spanish words not found in any dictionary, gesturing wildly. Ted just kept on walking down the street, his shoulders hunched. He never looked back.

Jim and I both laughed. "Hell," said Jim, glancing at me across the table, "it isn't just the language. It's a completely different view of the world, us and the locals. Things look familiar on the surface, and then we realize they're not. When I first arrived, I thought I had dropped off the edge of the world. The silence haunted me, especially at night. Good thing they gave me that book locker."

I looked over at the locker, standing upright, the narrow shelves holding paperback books of all sizes, and Jim smiled then shook his head at the memory of it all.

"For days and then weeks I sat down in the cantina, reading books, drinking too much beer, looking out the open door at the folks walking by, an occasional truck passing. Life like I never could've imagined. At first I was terrified and lonely. I swear, those books saved me. But then things changed. I read less and began talking to the people, all these amazing people, met the padre, became friends with the local doctor who visits once a month. Guy spends most of his time sewing up machete cuts. The campesinos come into town and drink too much beer and start disagreeing and out come the machetes."

Jim glanced over at me. "How long you been in-country?" he asked.

"Few months. Give or take. Seems longer."

"Don't worry. You'll get the hang of it. Just don't go home. More than a few in my group have. Some in yours will too. Probably a few already have. But stick. May take a year. But it's worth it. You won't believe how worth it. Help where you can, do a little good. You'll take more than you will ever give back. You'll never be the same. Hell, I'm worried when I get home it'll be like reverse culture shock. Being back there, in the world, probably it'll make my head hurt. Maybe my heart."

The next day we said goodbye. I never saw Jim again. Strangely, he was from Texas. From a much larger town called San Antonio. I returned to Bogotá on the red and yellow bus, the passengers stoic as we careened around corners and down steep hills, the tires howling, the dry wind blowing through the windows.

I never went back to San Antonio. I did take with me a few books from Jim's book locker, books I read and reread. I fell in love with certain characters and I relished the plots and the baroque descriptions of places I'd never been. Later I took an impossibly long train ride north, and seated on a hard bench I read for hours, a hefty novel by James Michener, *Hawaii*. It was wonderful.

DAY OF THE CALVES

Dr. Armando Canal looked at me for a long moment and smiled. We were finishing lunch at a restaurant near his office, sitting comfortably, sipping our coffee. "We have meat for the barrio program," he said. "Donated by a local rancher. All you have to do is arrange to have it picked up."

"Really? How much?"

"Five calves," he said. He took a cigarette from a flat case, tapped the tip on the case, and lit it with a silver lighter.

The barrio program was a type of Head Start for poor kids living on the outskirts of Bogotá, run by Colombians during the summer. Each day the kids got a hot meal of donated meat and vegetables and drinks. They played and colored and practiced their letters on large sheets of white paper and made papier-mache' masks and maps of Colombia.

On occasion, two CARE nurses came by and talked about hygiene and diet with those mothers who could attend. They even had a large plastic fly that they used as part of their presentation.

"Calves?" I said. "You mean veal, the meat wrapped and frozen. All I have to do is go and pick it up."

"Well, yes and no." Dr. Canal smiled, clearly savoring the moment. He was a businessman, a vice president of a Colombian company that manufactured terra cotta pipes and enormous water tanks. I had never seen him without a light-weight suit, white shirt, and dark tie or a stylish linen guayabera shirt. He had been educated at NYU and spoke unaccented English.

"Tell me."

"You will have to go and pick up the meat. It's not far from here. On a ranch, a finca. The calves are, however, alive."

"Alive?"

"Yes. You'll have them killed and butchered, wrapped in paper and refrigerated."

"You understand that the only meat I've ever seen was behind the glass of a meat counter, or wrapped in cellophane."

Dr. Canal took off his glasses and cleaned them with his napkin, trying for a serious look. "Of course. But five calves, that's a lot of meat for los niños. I have the name of a local butcher. He'll meet you at the finca of Don José Calderon on Friday. Mid-morning. You'll pay him 300 pesos. We've already settled on the price. He'll slaughter the calves, cut the meat and store it at his market in town where it can be picked up as needed."

We finished our coffee, and as we walked from the restaurant he handed me the directions to the finca. "The butcher's name is Raul. And be sure and let me know how it goes," he said. "The things we do, eh, gringo?"

He had always called me gringo, instead of Cristobal. But he used the word with affection. And on occasion I even referred to myself in conversation with the locals as a gringo, explaining that yes, indeed, we all came from Gringolandia. A place very close to Disneylandia. It never failed to make the Colombians smile. All I knew about the word, its etymology, so to speak, was that it came from Spain and meant, simply, foreigner, although some Latinos used it disparagingly.

That Friday I took one of the Peace Crops jeeps out to the finca, a two-hour drive. I stopped at a small café for coffee, a place with outdoor tables beneath a trellis of flowered vines. A large dog rested on the cool tiles near the entryway. A woman wearing an apron and white plastic sandals, her dark hair pulled back in a long braid, took my order and soon returned with a glass of water and a cup of coffee. I sipped my coffee and sat looking around, feeling the quiet, an occasional car passing by, a man across the street loading sacks of grain onto the bed of a hard-used pickup.

I knew I was delaying my arrival at the ranch and tried not to think about the calves.

Several men stood in front of a corner tienda, wooden crates of melons were stacked near the door. They slouched against the wall, smoking and talking, one ate something wrapped in white paper. A young boy, wearing shorts and a short-sleeve shirt, walked past me, selling lottery tickets and packets of Chiclets chewing gum. He slowed, eyeing me, uncertain, then headed toward the men across the street.

The finca was enormous, brown stubble grass and trees stretched to the horizon and black humpback cattle grazed in the distance.

A man I assumed was Raul stood by a weathered barn with a corral attached. A white stucco house with a red tile roof and wide porch was just beyond the turnaround driveway, flowers and fronds lined the walkway leading to the front porch, a spreading jacaranda tree heavy with blue blossoms was nearby.

I parked the jeep near the house, under the tree, and Raul waved me to the barn. He was a solidly built man, heavy through the shoulders, his face friendly, the color of mahogany, his hair grizzled. I introduced myself, and when we shook hands I could feel the burrs and calluses on the ridges of his palm.

We walked over to the corral and he gestured toward the calves. They were brown with white socks, long unsteady legs, and large suspicious eyes.

"So, here are the calves. Dr. Canal said you will use the meat for the children."

"Exactly." I handed him a white envelope with the pesos inside and he tucked it into his back pocket.

Raul walked back to the barn's opening and called in, "Hombres, vengan." Come.

Three men appeared, one carrying strands of rope, another with a long-bladed knife in a wooden scabbard.

"Well, Cristobal, we begin."

The men entered the corral by the gate and approached the calves. They bleated, letting out muted cries of apprehension, pushing against one another.

I stood there, my eyes narrowed, the sun intense, uncertain whether I wanted to watch, knowing only that the calves were about to be killed.

The men were talking casually as they caught the calves, threw them to the ground, and tied their hind legs. The calves struggled as if they intuited that the men, the dust, the strange hands holding them tightly, none of it would end well. When all of the calves were bound and lying on their sides, two men lifted a single calf and carried it to the side of the barn where they raised it by its hind legs, placing the tie rope over a large metal hook embedded in one of the overhanging rafters of the barn. Soon all the calves were hanging side by side on the hooks, strangely passive and quiet, their damp pink tongues protruding.

I wanted to leave or turn away, but I couldn't. I stood transfixed, gripping the top rail of the corral.

Everything seemed preternaturally quiet, and I thought of an afternoon some weeks back when I had been driving home on the outskirts of Bogotá. Cars and a local bus were stopped up ahead, and people had gathered on the sidewalk and in front of the bus. To the left was a Coca Cola truck, parked at an odd angle.

I slowed and then stopped. I asked a woman, standing near the curb, what had happened. She shrugged impassively, and when I didn't look away explained that a Coca Cola truck had hit a man. "He was on a bicycle, turned in front of the truck and was killed."

I drove closer, looking for escape down a side street, when I noticed that the dead man, young, perhaps in his teens, had been hung by his torn shirt on a row of empty bottles standing upright in their wooden crates. It appeared as if he was leaning against the truck, his head at an odd angle, his arms hanging limply in front of him, his eyes glazed. A man was taking his picture. Children crowded around the photographer who stood hunched forward, looking through the lens of the camera.

The woman's shrug summed up an attitude, one that said that life and death were part of a continuum. People would mourn for the young man, his mother would lament and weep, but there was also a resignation that could easily be misinterpreted as indifference.

I watched as Raul took the knife from the wooden scabbard and ran his thumb along the edge of the blade. Satisfied, he approached the first calf. Holding it by one ear, he pulled back the head, exposing the neck, and cut quickly through the hide. A stream of blood spilled onto the ground. The calf never made a sound. Raul then walked to the next calf and did the same thing until all the calves were bleeding out, pools of dark coagulating blood glistening in the late morning sun.

I noticed, off to my left, in the direction of the house, an elderly woman carrying an enamel pitcher and large cup, running toward the barn and the calves.

She pushed through the gate into the corral and held the pitcher under one of the calves and the cup under another, smiling first at Raul and then at me. "Hierro," she said. Iron. "La sangre tiene vitaminas." The blood has vitamins. She drank from the cup while moving the pitcher from one calf to the next. She had a crescent of dark red blood on her upper lip and she wiped it away with the back of her hand.

Raul stood cleaning his knife with a soiled rag, paying no attention to the woman. I looked off toward the mountains in the distance, the horizon lost in a haze of dust and sunshine. I was a very long way from home.

LA ESCOBA DE DIOS

For a time I lived in a residencia in Cartagena. It was a two-story stucco place with a generous front porch lined with chairs. In the evenings, the boarders sat comfortably on the porch smoking cigars, some sipping final cups of coffee and talking about the day. The trade winds, balmy and soft, were a welcome relief from the unrelenting heat of the day.

They were businessmen, some local, others worked in Cartagena during the week and then traveled home on weekends to be with their families. None of the men were simply passing through. They had their own rooms, took meals together, and some developed friendships over time.

There was a woman who cleaned the residencia, a Señora Sanchez. She was an older woman, always shrouded in black, her heavy stockings rolled down just below her knees, her hair the color of ash, always pulled back severely and held in place by a tortoise shell comb. She carried a white handkerchief pushed up under one sleeve, and whenever she paused before a window she would pat her forehead and cheeks with it. She rarely smiled, her face inscrutable, as if she were thinking of something else.

I asked Mike, a Colombian friend and one of the residents, about Señora Sanchez. Why was she so stern and silent?

Mike, or Miguel as I called him, who spoke passable English, had gone to school in Boston where he studied engineering and had recently returned to Cartagena to head the Public Utilities Department. He said she carried la escoba de Dios, the broom of God. I had never heard the expression before. We were sitting across from one another at the long dining room table, drinking the last of our morning coffee, sunlight filling the room.

"La escoba de Dios," I repeated, pausing, curious. But thinking about the señora, I asked, "Why always a black dress?"

Miguel told me that she had lost her husband and was in a period of mourning.

"Really," I said. "It must be hard coming to work each day having just lost your husband."

"Well," said Miguel, "not *just* lost her husband. It's been some time."

"How long?" I asked.

"I would say... of course I am not certain... some twenty years."

"Twenty years? They must have been very close."

"Perhaps," he said. "It is a thing difficult to know."

I looked at him and I assumed he was thinking about Señora Sanchez and her years of suffering and loss. But I heard something else in his voice.

"Wait, Miguel, tell me, how can one explain twenty years of black dresses if they weren't close?"

He considered my question then said, "This is not an easy thing. Let me say that her grief has become, well, something else. My opinion? I think she wears the black dress to remind herself that God is just and fair and all forgiving and she must be respectful. But for Señora Sanchez, herself? Personally? She will never forget and never forgive."

"Forgive what?" I asked.

"It was a tragic and terrible thing," said Miguel.

"What?" I asked.

He paused and picked up a glass saltshaker, turning it in his hand, passing the flat of his thumb along its corrugated sides.

"Mike," I said in English. "What was so terrible?"

"The passing of Señor Sanchez."

"Señor Sanchez. But what does his death have to do with forgiving? Dying was not his fault," I said.

"Well, no, of course not, but... Without a doubt, Señor Sanchez, he was a fine and distinguished gentleman, a civil servant of great instincts, a man once responsible for the utility, where I work today. However, he died in a most unfortunate way. It was his heart. The walls, they were like fine tissue paper. Whenever he smoked a cigar, his lips would turn the slightest blue.

"The day of his untimely passing, I am told he was out for a walk, something he often did in the late afternoon, and unexpectedly collapsed on the street. As it happened, he was in front of the apartment of the widow Señora Sandoval, thankfully a nurse many years ago, in Spain I think, and much experienced in such matters. She found him on the sidewalk in great distress, and took him inside and made him comfortable in her bed until the doctors could arrive. But by then, well, it was too late. Nothing could be done. A great and unexpected tragedy."

Miguel looked at me knowingly, nodding his head. As if all had now been made clear.

I looked at him, waiting, saying, "And...?"

"And so," he continued, "Señora Sanchez cleans our residencia as if she were cleaning and sweeping with la escoba de Dios. She pounds our shirts on the stone slab until the collars are frayed – I would recommend you take your shirts to Señora Cruz, she has a small laundry down by the ocean. Perhaps her husband is still alive."

Jaime grinned, then said, "So you see, Cristobal, Señora Sanchez bangs the pots and pans, breaks the china, and often boils the eggs until they are like small rubber balls. She dusts the furniture and cleans the floors and she makes the morning coffee of such strength that it must be doused with milk and sugar or it will make your eyes water. Everything she does, even riding the bus, she does with great dignity and grief. She is a most wonderful widow. None has ever done it better."

Miguel stood and walked over to a window, looking out at something in the distance, his expression thoughtful. He turned and glanced back at me, saying, "One can only assume it gives her peace and gratification for she has been this way for twenty years. Such a thing. I heard a priest say that somewhere in her silence and abiding anger she has found a redemptive forgiveness. The widow who carries la escoba de Dios."

Miguel came back to the table and finished his coffee and we talked of other things until he left for the utility.

Each day, just as the sun was pushing back the gray of dawn, Señora Sanchez appeared at the residencia carrying a heavy nylon bag, a small leather purse, and a look of unapproachable silence. I often heard her walking heavily around the kitchen, drawers pulled open, the sounds of silverware being sorted, dishes put away, and the pungent smell of coffee announcing her presence long before I ever saw her. If we met in the early morning I would always say, "Buenos dias, Señora. Café listo?" Is the coffee ready? And she would nod and gesture with her hand toward the kitchen and walk away. We rarely spoke.

I wondered what she said to Señor Sanchez in the first moments of the day, and even asked Miguel what he thought. He looked at me and smiled. We could only imagine, but, of course, we will never know.

BOBBY

It was late in the afternoon. Señora Sanchez knocked on my door and told me that I had a call from Miguel and I could use the phone in his room. The residencia didn't have a common telephone.

Though we had become friends over the months I had lived at the residencia, I had never been in his room. The bed was made, and the neatness of the room surprised me. Miguel's phone was heavy and black with a rotary dial, and sat on a nightstand near his bed.

"Miguel, hi," I said. "Qué pasa?"

He answered me in English.

"Cristobal, I just heard, and I'm very sorry."

"Sorry about what?" I said.

"You don't know? Damn. It's a great lastima. Bobby Kennedy was killed in Los Angeles. Earlier today. It came over the news, here at the utility. I know you were hopeful he might be president."

Because Miguel had spent years in Boston, we often sat at the dining room table and talked about America, his decision to return to Cartagena, about the Kennedy brothers, and earlier that spring, the assassination of Martin Luther King. 1968 had already been an awful, wrenching year, the loss of MLK an event that sent paroxysms of grief and anger through cities, coast to coast.

"Oh, God," I said. "Killed? How?"

"I'm not sure," he said. "Reports are that he was shot in Los Angeles, at a hotel. He won the California primary and was leaving, after giving a speech. Someone shot him. In a kitchen, I think. That's all I know."

I stood very still, looking out the window, seeing nothing, feeling an anguish that broke my heart. I was thousands of miles away and I longed to be there, to understand what happened.

Bobby. Bobby Kennedy. I had followed his nascent campaign for the presidency with hope and anticipation. I had seen images of him standing in the back of a convertible, Rafer Johnson's and Rosey Grier's arms wrapped around him as they drove through some of the toughest neighborhoods in Los Angeles, people spilling out onto the street, hands outstretched, hoping to make contact, to brush his leg, to touch his hand, and Bobby, waving, pushing back his shock of hair, grinning that amazing boyish grin.

Bobby died the next morning, June 6, 1968, at the Good Samaritan Hospital, 82 days after he had started his campaign for the presidency. He had brought with him, wherever he spoke, a renewed hope and conviction that deeply moved those who heard him. He had spoken eloquently and passionately after Martin was assassinated and he had pleaded for calm.

His body was flown back to New York City where he lay in state at Saint Patrick's Cathedral. Several days later, a funeral train took his coffin from New York to Washington D.C. for burial at Arlington Cemetery. It was a remarkable, memorable journey.

I watched some of it on a small black and white television in a local bar not far from the docks. I sat at a table alone, a beer in front of me, and waited for the evening news to be broadcast out of Bogotá. In Spanish, of course.

Some men were sitting at the bar, a few at tables, most were talking or reading newspapers. I had asked the bartender to turn up the volume when the news came on and I sat holding my breath, desperate for something. For anything.

That was when I saw, briefly, the stark images of the funeral train passing through the countryside, through towns large and small, the tracks lined with hundreds and thousands of mourners, some with young children, hands raised, bidding Bobby farewell. Others stood very still, grief etched on their faces.

Sitting there in the dim light of early evening, I could feel my throat tighten, my eyes stinging with emotion. I mourned for Bobby Kennedy, and I mourned for the fact that I was so far from home. I wanted desperately to be there, to add my grief to that of the nation, to share in the collective sadness that would be, as with Martin, beyond consolation.

Weeks later, seated at a table in the Vista Del Mar, Señora Cruz watching me discretely as she ironed, I wrote Ted Kennedy a brief note of regret, struggling to find just the right words. Unexpectedly, I received a black-bordered card in return, thanking me for my letter of condolence. In simple script was written the following: *He who learns must suffer. And even in our sleep pain that cannot forget falls drop by drop upon the heart, and in our own despair, against our will, comes wisdom to us by the awful grace of God. – Aeschylus*

I showed the card to Miguel, explaining that it came from Edward Kennedy. That I had written him. He read it slowly and passed it back to me. There was nothing more to say and we left the dinner table and walked out onto the front porch of the residencia and sat down with the other men who were talking quietly. It had started to rain, a soft rain, and the air smelled like newly mown grass. And while I sat there in the early evening with those Colombian men, I looked out at the wet and I was glad I was there. Out in the all of it.

To Robert Murillo, WCR, amigo mio, with gratitude for his time and support.

ABOUT THE AUTHOR

Chris Honoré is a freelance journalist based in Ashland, Oregon. He was a Peace Corps Volunteer in Colombia, South America.

www.ingramcontent.com/pod-product-compliance
Lightning Source LLC
Chambersburg PA
CBHW050336290526
45785CB00006B/2513